My Name Is Another Word

Beth Wood

SMALL POND
PUBLISHING

My Name Is
Another Word

Beth Wood

TABLE OF CONTENTS

3. AND SO I RISE

For the builders and the dreamers.
Don't you ever forget.

"You have always been the place.
   You are a woman who can build it yourself.
   You are born to build."
                    --Sarah Kay "The Type"

My Name Is Another Word

Beth Wood

LITTLE QUEEN, LITTLE DIAMOND

I dreamed this poem
and you were in it;

flying above the singing trees
and the rolling river full of fish,
next to the laughing goose
(who all by himself did seem silly),
we were weightless and giggling
with butter-colored paper mâché wings.

Look, there's the memory house,
you said.
Yep, and I raced you
to the edge of a rainbow.

For all of our soarings and tumblings,
no one noticed down on earth—
too busy staring at their screens to see
two kindreds on a Tuesday
flying free like falcons,
like renegade balloons.

Little Queen, I said,
Little Diamond, can you hear me?
Let's make a world.

The Memory House

MY NAME IS ANOTHER WORD

The place where I was born
smells of cow shit and dust,
bruise-colored thunderheads holding
court on the yawning far horizon.
In the wee hours one spring morning
my mother labored me here, cried
as they whisked away my tiny body,
hooked me up to machines, the sudden
world I had parachuted into searing
my paper-thin eggshell eyelids.
I opened my mouth like a hungry bird.
It is a singular blessing that my mother
loves birds. My grandmother stepped
on a scorpion one night; another night,
one took up residence in her nightgown.
She rubbed a paste of meat tenderizer on
her wounds, made biscuits, carried on—
pistol under her mattress, curled up
rattlesnake under the porch, the smell
of bacon cooking on cast iron, strong
coffee from a can in the morning.
If I were strong, I would carry on.
I would hold the world in my arms—
even the stinging parts.
I would fold grandmother, mother
into my marrow; I would build
a scaffolding. I think my name
is another word for house
(correct me if I'm wrong);
no one ever told me what it means.

THE WINGS

We don't speak of it
and so are left to wonder
where it came from:

Was it really there?
Did it really happen?
Forged in heat and dust

and dark leather and
clouded jars in the old
leaning junk barn,

I could hear it
like faraway music—
I could feel it on my skin.

You're just sensitive,
the wholeworld would say
screeching to a halt;

shame was built for this—
repackaged and reworked,
its rust soaked in humorless

vinegar. By the hours too dim
for language, she emerged
a wet and shimmering moth;

I took the wings.
I flew.

SPEAKING PLAIN(S)

What does it make me
if I say it plain? I did not
come here to obfuscate.

I smile in wonder at the
sophisticate, the connoisseur
of high art untouched

by savage light, the
gilded high architecture
of a snake eating its tail.

I prefer horses standing
in a field of swaying grass
at the exact moment sun

heaves a sigh: barbed wire
its own grand score
transposing the West

into a minor key. There
was other music once.
Nod if you can hear it.

THE CARRYING

Commune with nature,
they say, producing rivers
of books and articles
about the health benefits
of "forest bathing," rewilding,"
making up words for what
we have done to ourselves,
what we are trying to undo.
While any child could tell you
who has climbed up a tree
sipping hours, watching a moth
dance with helicopter wind,
touching its powdery wings
with a single fingertip:
your you-ness becomes
borderless, small; blue
sky sings invitation, then
pirouettes into evening.
Running home to make it
just in time for dark, you
just might carry a world—
not for shoulders, not
like a weight: like a seed.

ARMIES

Oh, thank youuuu! but I always
wanted straight hair hahaha!

and the toothpick legs, too
    and the flat chest,

the kind of face that looks
    pretty while sleeping.

I wanted a Barbie waist
    way up high and cinched,

walking on tiptoes dreaming
    of pink spike platform shoes

that would bring me closer
    to tall (but not *too* tall).

I wanted to erase my plump,
    loud, freckled self.

How many of us? And for what?
    Armies of subtraction wasting

the sweet fruit of our dreaming
    on this: decade after spinning

decade lived in pencil,
    trying to get back on the page.

ANGER IS A HAMMER AND WHERE
IS THE NAIL

I don't know how to be angry. It's a
southern girl thing, I'm not joking,
although it sounds funny when I say it.
It just wasn't polite, you know. Now
I sit with it like a hammer in my chest
and I can't dissolve it, yank it, polish it,
or even find the handle. All else melts
away and it remains—salt from the
ocean, gun powder, residue. If I pick
it up and use it, I'm throwing hammers.
I would say *I'm sorry* to put feathers
back in place, but I'm not. Still, feathers
should be smooth, shouldn't they? Look
away, child, look away. We wouldn't
want the neighbors to talk. A hammer
has its place, as does a nail.

BY THE POOL

I don't know how to stop
numbing
drumming fingers
humming to myself

can't stop crunching
munching
lunching alldamn day

salty things
no thing sweet
a pithy tweet here
there and everywhere

She's not to be believed
her body language
her mouth language

I can't stop scrolling
rolling
trolling for answers

for one sane moment
to hold on to
sing along to
get gone to

I remember the boy-man
cop who forgot
and accidentally brought

his gun to the airport,
hair barely long enough to
shave, save

the snide remarks for later
by the pool
acting cool he said

'Nice stretchmarks!'
about my thighs,
my eyes got SO big

this barely grown
peachfuzz fuzz
telling me my body

was wrong. I carried it
for so long, he must
be right, right?

I remember thinking
yeah, I may be ugly,
but we shouldn't give guns

to children.

IN LIEU OF FLOWERS,

keep the moon,
her Hollywood teeth
beaming that delicious
trickster smile spilling
me into waterfall joy,
I can't help it, I want
her flashlight forever.

Stop the nights
and the renegade days
so that everything hovers
untouched, bone silent.

Leave the dishes.
It is a strange thing
to love the dust.

Send the rain,
let grass bloom thick
in spring, kelly green
velvet, perfect for
tender feet, paws
to walk on, soft
bodies to lie in.

Send the words,
all of them, and when
their buzz is gone,
send some more.
Conjure them, find
them, go searching.

There was never
a better doorway
to yesterday—and
once the shining
moon goes, to the un-
fathomable tomorrow.

A SOFT KIND OF MERCY

One year ago we were
on the floor, I thought,
the memory so distant
that a silver flash just now
sent me flying backwards.

I was painting toenails,
rearranging little papers,
playing *watch-this-disappear!*
Anything to be near
you, to hear your breath.

My knowing knew you
were slipping away, my
un-knowing was the last
to know. At the water's
edge I threw all the rocks

back in, heard the circles
splash, said *See? We're here!*
out loud. You waited until
I was asleep to go. A soft
kind of mercy—only

old souls know how.
The page turned swiftly,
left me baffled and bereft,
pulling on shadows until

my arms went numb.

Sorrow made a seed of me;
then it rained.

NO DIRECTION

For the hard things
    there are no instructions,

yet here are pages and pages
    of illustrations for the easy ones.

Yes, I know how to operate
    a coffeemaker, and yes, even

a curling iron, thank goodness
    for the heat warnings!

I live on the edge as I recycle
    the booklet for the crockpot.

Page after page of cartoony
    mansplaining in every flowery

language, but nothing at all
    of creeping sorrow,

unnamed dread. No direction
    when it comes to you on a raft

drifting away before I can reach
    the solid shore.

THE EMPTY CHAIR

You could look at the empty chair and say
    Bless all who have rested here.

You could look at the empty chair and say
    Bless those who have not known rest.

You could look at the empty chair and say
    Praise the wood, the forest, the trees.

You could look at the empty chair and say
    Praise the blade, the hammer, the artisan.

You could look at the empty chair and say
    Praise the emptiness.

You could look at the empty chair and say
    My feet hurt.

You could look at the empty chair and say
    No, you sit.

You could look at the empty chair and say
    Thank you.

You could look at the empty chair and say
    nothing

        and you would all be right.

RIVER KEEPER
after Anis Mojgani

Oh littleheart,
beat the drum.
River keeper,
keep your center.
Remember there is
great electricity
behind you—don't
let anyone call you
a machine. For
the times you have
spoken, interrupted
my stunned silence,
I thank you. For
the times I have
forgotten you,
I bow down. It's
not easy being
animal. But wait—
it IS, you say? You
are always saying
something, like
a sticky child at
the table who blurts
out profoundly wise
words that shake
awake these rusty
sleepers. Just now,

the sky reinvents
itself. Hats off
to you, little one;
beat the drum.

ALMOST HOLY

I combed the dusty bookshop
for treasures, zeroing in on "Used Poetry"
which caused my heart to sing, because
what good is poetry if it is not used?
The book on "poetry as spiritual practice"
caught my eye, hoping under my breath
for *spirit* of the lower-case kind.
In school before choir concerts
and spelling bees they would lead us
in prayer, my particular kind of prayer
being to stare out the window and wait
for this awkward ritual to pass like weather.
Why speak to singing children
of shadows and death? Why other me
and my friend with the burnt caramel
skin who just shrugged her shoulders
when our eyes met? (We formed a secret
club who perfected the skill of looking
as if we were reciting the Lord's Prayer—
we should have made matching t-shirts:
"Fakers Unite!" "Almost Holy!")
I am delighted to find the book is
signed by the author with tender words:
Dear Rosemary – with blessings always,
and gratitude for the work you do…
I can almost feel her with me now
in this blooming morning before the sun
scales the mountain, our tall cousin; with

the taste of coffee on my tongue I whisper,
Rosemary, where did you go?
Rosemary, why all of this othering?

MOTHER

Mother,
I don't know how
to tell you this.
All week I have listened
by the river, all week I have
floated on this idea, then
that one, fashioning myself
into a quiet observer with salty
almonds and ripe juicy cherries
in her bag to kill the hunger.
The always hunger. I'm tap
dancing now while I watch
this dragonfly. What I'm trying
to say is she is with me here,
you are with me, but that isn't
everything. You already know
that much. What I'm saying is
I heard words in a whisper, I
wrote them down, only to find
them later tumbling directly
from someone else's mouth.
Like my knowing knew what
would happen before it happened,
just like hers used to do, like
holding an invisible rope.
Mother, what I'm trying to say is
I won't let go.

LET ME TELL YOU
  after Bob Hicok, "A Primer"

On the high plains where
we know how to lie flat,
the horizon is something we're
held by, not looking for. Let
me tell you about the smell
of cow shit, wide cotton fields
strung together like a run-on
sentence, the howling dust-devil
that picked up our Volkswagen
Beetle one day while we were in it
and placed us squarely on the other
side of the road like an egg
that got dropped but didn't break.
Let me tell you of the surprised look
on my mother's face, the nervous
laughter that erupted after we
crashed down, "Slip Slidin Away"
playing on the radio, the tumbleweed
that served as exclamation point.
Which reminds me—our state
motto is "I tell you what!"
Old timers drove their Cadillac
boats down brick streets bumping
through town. The rich paunchy ones
were called Cattle Men, the poor
skinny ones, cowboys. You'll notice
there are ghosts in this scene.
Our state bird is a rodeo clown;
no trees to hold the dirt down and so
it flew with the wind in a symphony

of muted hues, sky pregnant and
smudged with wild rose, smelling
of something burning far away.
To watch a prairie dog arguing with
her neighbor, the burrowing owl—
a quiet joy. A thundershower on your
sun-scorched skin: cause for dancing.
Hey, y'all look I found a horny toad! No,
YOU hold it, brother! I was the one
who collected quiet joys, placed them
in my music box; all these whirling
years later, I am still collecting.
What I want to offer up is this:
You take it with you.
You leave it behind.
Tell me about the places
you are leaving.

Reason Enough

THE BEST CONVERSATIONS

The best conversations
are round, no sharp

corners, so true you can
navigate by them at night.

A touchpoint here and
there in a life scattered,

weathered, seemingly
left to chance. Walking

through the woods
you find a deep cave—

you can shelter there, be-
tween ceilingdrips dream

of all those who have
sheltered there before

in the thick green
canopy of language.

The best ones fit in
your pocket, smooth

stones for thumbing,
tiny objects you might

forget but still come
from the wash singing.

And I'll tell you it's
not just with humans.

Once the winding water
asked me *who is there?*

and I said *I'm still learning.*
Once, grandmother moon said

child, where are you going?
and I said *I'm still learning.*

The sky will tell you what she's
thinking before she says it.

A spotted horse at the fence—
his field of wavinggrass

stretching on forever, his
brown eye an orb filled with

ancient knowing, not-knowing
said *But why have you come?*

and I said *I'm still learning,
and aren't you lonely?*

Yes, he said, and he nodded,
swished. I touched the star

between his eyes, he sighed.
I said *so am I*.

DAMMIT, I'M TRYING TO BE BITTER

Have you ever stepped into the garden
with sleepyfeet and bedhead doing your best
to remember how to be grateful for all of it?

The mud, the shit, the sudden unwelcome
pellets of hail even while cucumber vines
climb like impossible arms toward the

leaning gate for the sake of the sun?
You try your best not to gasp at the fragile
beauty of morning dew, its tilt just right

for lighting up shimmering waterdrops on
flower petals. *But this pebble lodged in my heart*,
you say. A new blossom smaller than

a pinprick says *yes, exactly that, yes.*

WONDERING WHY SOME PEOPLE THINK POETRY IS SCARY

In my trusty notebook I wrote,
"Poetry asks us to go below the surface;
for this reason it is disruptive."

And I know I'm not the one
to start movements or lead marches.
I'm not the fiery, flashy leader

with more hope than answers.
But I can raise my hand
from the back of the classroom

and when called upon say
This moment is gold,
your beating heart a treasure.
Don't you ever forget.

WHEN WE SAY BEACON
  —for Amanda Gorman

When we say beacon
we mean lighthouse,
light-bringer, singer of light.
We mean laser beam,
signal fire, spitfire
warbling in a yellow coat.
We mean spark of boldness
we never dared to imagine,
knifecold bright morning sun
shouting suddenly *I'm here!*
We mean call and response
and you're calling us now.
We mean bird of hope
winging, finding us in our lost
and lonely places, scattering
melody as if to say *yes children,*
it's here, and it never stops at all.

POETRY AT THE SUPER BOWL

"Poetry at the Super Bowl"
is a phrase I never thought
I'd hear, except perhaps as
a headline in *The Onion,*
or to describe the ballet-like
caress of a 300-lb tank of a
man who floated a catch in
the end zone as if his hands
were made of flower petals.
But now I hear the real words
and they shimmer like quick-
dawn gold edging this winter
horizon. Hang on. "Madame
Vice President" robbed me
of my breath and caused me
to wonder what-on-earth else
glorious awaits us? That we
never thought we'd see? Oh
my stars. My imagination can
surely do better. All of ours
now. Until then I'll keep
picking my jaw up off the
floor, snapping photos of
bright new flowers budding
young in between the
cracks, blooming my worn-
out notion of hope
into something I can
dream on.

TO THE DARK-EYED JUNCO SCRATCHING
OUTSIDE MY WINDOW

How do you know
when to stop,
where to scratch,
when to flit over
to another patch of dirt?
How do you know
where the seeds will be?
The mosquitos?
How do you divide time,
please forgive me,
do you?
What unnamable compass
feathered you here under
my window?
How do you grieve
when the thief raccoon
comes, raids your nest,
when your children fall
and lie crumpled, still
wearing their transparent
skin? How do you get up
and do it all over again?
However you weep,
I weep.
For the blind miracle
of being alive,
for losing it all.

THE YOUNG PEOPLE

The young people don't
    wear makeup. They dress
        like lumberjacks, farmers,
            mustardy thick wool hats
            and lug-soled boots,
                cropped-off flannel in the rain.

They have the nerve
    to appear, dare I say it,
        plain while carrying on
            conversations, carrying baby on hip,
                carrying an unnamable weight,
                    carrying reusable mugs full of tea.

They have thoughts
    and opinions, fully expressed.
        They make things.
            Do business, grow, fail,
                eat, weep, function, dream,
                    make beautiful

a small patch of the world.
    This gives me more hope than
        legislation, litigation,
            proclamation, declaration.
                Bless this exquisite tilt.
                    Bless this leaning toward love.

ANY ORDINARY MINUTE

The animal inside each of us
breathes synchronous, happy
camouflage of heartbeat
nestled next to heartbeat.
For that woman on the corner
it's a crow, picking up a penny
to turn it over, rub it for luck.
Inside a past lover was
a smooth-skinned frog,
leaping and leaping from
one desire to another,
the heron in my chest
bone-silent, thin, resolute.
I see in the bent-over old
man a startled horse, lean
and hungry. With a crooked
smile I cheer him on—
any ordinary minute
he might slip away
and go for broke.

SOMETHING IT WAS

These are the days
of making something
out of nothing;

these are the days
of *well, we tried.*

These are the days
of eyes searching,
half-smirks, grimaces,
smiles hidden behind cloth.

These are the days
of skin shedding,
tending roots,
garnering faith like wheat
for the winter.

These are the days
of not knowing,
of knowing we do not know.
The blankness of it,
and the fullness.

Scattered light days,
palindrome days
on the cusp;
hold my hand while we
peek over the edge.

Someday we will lock
eyes and both say
Wasn't that something.

REASON ENOUGH

If you feel like a broken record
telling your story, just remember
the quiet bubbling hallelujah sound
of birds warbling before rising time,

each new day a treasure to announce.
Does anyone tell a sparrow to stop
babbling? Does anyone say *hey, you told
that one already.* Does anyone begrudge

the melody? *I'm here, I'm here, I'm here,*
you say. It's morning. We survived
the darkness once again, come closer.
Reason enough for a song.

PINK MOON MORNING

Spring is offering
her breast, and our
thirst bears shriveled-
up fruit, an asking like
never before. On the
winding drive to a
friend's riverhouse,
wind flaps the dogs'
ears like tiny velvety
sails; late sun kindles
heat on my exposed
neck just like your lips
brushing them in the
pink moon morning.
We stand around ten
feet from each other
laughing nervously,
hugging air, lamenting
our failure of language,
how time and again
we've done violence
to it. All of us strung
out, weirded out, miss-
ing out, lonely in our
bones, all of us ready
to drink.

MY LOVE WHOM I LOVE TO LOVE

he calls me, and whimsy
curls around my fingers;
I braid a tiny basket of it.

My love whom I lovingly love to love,
I add, grinning with my cattail
teeth, let's play with

conjugation, let's improvise
with paint, throw words on
canvas, turn around to see

this bucolic scene unfolding.
Trickster autumn hands out
cards: Warm, Sunny, Golden,

then Cold, Stormy; she throws
the whole deck into the wind.
Let's follow this trail by the

singing swirling river, deep
and ancient but new just now,
to remember how we got here.

Now the dogs at home are snug
in their beds napping, snoring
or taking inventory

or dreaming of some wild thing
to chase, asleep like our love was
before we discovered the wonder

of it, before we took into our
hands the verb of it, before by
saying it, we made it so.

EVERYDAY RIVERSONG

This morning
when light was just blushing,
they drifted in, drifted out—
white pelicans exhausted from
their journey. A silent cotton
monolith, bobbing flotilla
skimming these fertile waters
for an easy meal.

I wanted to cry it was so hopeful.
I wanted to sing a song they recognized.
I wanted to imagine any one of us
can keep our sorrow private,
hidden in the reeds.

Yet here they are
holding formation,
moving without a sound.
How does the song go?
Every day it's the same.

Even if we never arrive,
we're going somewhere.
Even if we never arrive,
none of us migrates
alone.

LOOKING UP AT DEAD DEER HEADS IN A
MOUNTAIN-TOWN LODGE
COFFEEHOUSE

When I say the back
of my teeth hurt staring
up at this, you might
know what I mean.
In line when I hum
a silky song skating just
underneath my breath,
it might spark a memory,
tender or fraught, in places
I can't see, places where
you're barely hanging on.
Music whispers to us that
way, to our animal skin.
On our haunches we wait
for the next grieving thing—
scent of new day in the air,
scent of weathered promises:
a life stuffed into the corner.
The taxidermy of meaning,
gentle sawdust of regret.

MY DOG HANNAH AND THE
NEED-TO-KNOW BASIS

For days she has been craving it,
her nose upturned and sifting air,
searching, arrowing in.

Last week our peaceful morning
was shattered by a doe in the throes
of death, standing then falling,

dragging herself to the edge of our pond,
her neck becoming a still and twisted rope.
Something else dragged her off in the night.

Ravens had their way, an eagle muscled
in, geese laughing refused to answer
the question of where they are going,

and will they ever arrive? This morning
I relented, let her blinding curiosity lead us,
and despite all the days and winds gone by,

she walked right up to the twisted rope
spot, devouring every detail, drinking
every wiff of every wisp of memory

of coarse dun hair, sinking her nose in
until her face was buried in deep brown
goo and mud and humus and answers.

What a mess, I thought, but how can I
blame her? Ravenous for the story
and how it ends.

AS LONG AS THERE IS MYSTERY

To the questions
that have no answers,
I salute you.

Mute eyes of a fuzzy doe
standing in a field,
chewing sideways.

Invisible wind washing
this moment clean,
daring me to notice

a bright bluebird on the
fencepost puffed up with
asking. *What is it?* I say.

It's hard to feel lonely
when there is so much
delicious mystery

and the answers
are just beyond reach.
A hawk circles, weaving

spiderweb shadows.
It is hard to feel lonely
if you are listening.

DIFFERENT ONES

It is hard to believe
how much time it takes
an old lady carrying a big bag
to make it to row 28F on an
airplane and then try to raise
her bag above her head—
a bird with clipped wings.

The pilot checks his watch.
Behind her a mom
hikes a baby onto her hip.

Here, let me help, says a kind
stranger with a baseball cap.

Oh thank you! she exclaims—
breathless, plopping into
her seat with an *Ooomf!*
She says to the air, *Goodness,
my holding-on muscles are tired.*

No one nods,
there is no answer.

I think: there are different ones
for letting go.

CONVERSATION WITH SPEED

If I run faster, sticky time will release itself
from the burnt edges of grandmother's cast
iron pan.

     Nope, that's not it.

If I run faster, the haunching midnight cat
of my borderless grief will bound out and
never get caught.

     Not quite it.

If I run faster, my forgetting will fan out like
spilled water, filling every crack, pulled by
the moon to flow downhill and join a larger
version of itself.

     Hardly.

If I run faster, the years will think I'm funny.

     Now we're getting somewhere.

If I run faster, my hope wakes up, becomes
a wheel.

     Closer.

If I run faster, I join the wind.

     Yes.

If I sit still, I also join the wind.

Indeed.

I'll go fetch my shoes.

I KNOW THE FEELING

There's a bird trapped in the garage.
I am alarmed, bereft; it is midnight,
I am heavy-lidded, sleepy, cooked.
Flutterflutter against the wall,
the ceiling, he cannot find the door,
I know the feeling.

I'm so tired I think I'll just
go to bed and hope he gets out
when the door is on its way down.
I sleep the sleep of one who knows
there's a bird trapped in the garage.
I go out first thing, all is quiet, *aha*
I think, he finally found his way.

Then in a whir of feathers and dust
he is Tasmanian devilling again.
I recognize his thirst, hunger, panic,
the night spent alone, the chance he
missed when he forgot his magnificent
bird self.
I know the feeling.

I open both doors wide and only
after I say out loud *Hey! Friend!*
does he find the sky waiting,
I know the feeling.
He flies away.

BE STILL

my leaning heart,
and give me strength to know
I will survive this longing.

Be brave my tired feet
and trust this body
to know which waves to take
head on,
which to ride to the top,
which to duck under
(trickster moon).

These are corduroy days
and building blocks,
drum kits and sticky
pancake plates.

Memory lives here in every
thread of this couch, every
surface and yet time
leans forward, we grow
tipsy with these
seesaw dreams.

Go ahead: bite an orange. Sip
from the vines of golden valleys,
savor, turn
toward sun.

THE GATE

It will come late
or it will come early—
in the middle of the night
or on the here-and-there train.

It will come while
you're not looking,
sliding in sideways like
a glance;

it will come frequently
enough to quench your thirst,
then stay away long enough
to tease it.

Lying down, it feels
like a curtain of warm
saltwater, sitting up
like forgiving rain.

Maybe it comes while
chopping onions,
while walking around
the going-nowhere lake,

while hearing a baby cry
or remembering something.
Maybe it will come while
washing your hair, taking

out the trash, letting go
behind-the-dam tears so
your heart may become
loose again.

If you are lucky,
while holding a pen.
You see? A dream works both
ways. Leave the gate open.

And So I Rise

THE DREAM

I woke up from a dream
where I went round and round,

crisscrossed here and there
trying to prove my belonging

to a world as indifferent
as water, as wind.

Dizzy, confused,
I searched for solid ground

hovering just above these
singing trees with a thirst

I no longer recognized.
My suitcase gathered dust.

I buried the plans
for the house my sorrow built.

Winter's hymn was an owl
who said *keep listening;*

spring was a concerto of bees
spinning longing into fuel.

All this time thinking
I had lost something

I was finding it. All this time
I was sharpening the blade.

62

SUDDEN TEARS (IN THE SOUTH)

I thought I was over it, then distant
music triggered a memory that stings
my nose, crinkles my foreheard,
sends waterfalls down my face.
Try as I may to forget my mouth
will not let me, nor will my ears.
I once heard our senses are a gateway,
but to what? To the empty field where
the dirt-covered hole holds the box
with the key in it? Every tear is a surprise
visitor I can welcome – *oh, helloooo!* –
at least someone knows where I live.
In the South you make room
for strangers, even unannounced.
You make gallon jugs of sun tea, tiny
triangle pimento cheese sandwiches,
lemon cookies dusted with fine sugar;
you feed them like family. Maybe
some rituals are a proving ground.
Maybe it was all practice for this.

WHAT IF I SAID

What if I said
Poetry is everywhere!
You might say,
but check the glove box,
and I would say,
exactly. Whispering lilies
sprouted from sand,
burnt sky falling halfway
around the world; both
things radiating light
at the same time, both
things astonishing.
I want to say
Poetry is everywhere!
even on the internet.
In the mouth of the tired
bus driver—*sit down children,*
sit doooooown please. In the
seashell curl of a newborn's
ear, at the bottom of this
muddy singsong pond,
frogs waking up.
Wait right here; listen.
A cloud will say it true,
then the rain.

HOW DO I KNOW

How do you know
if it will be a poem
or a song? is a question
I am asked the most.

Answer: it is how they
arrive. A song
is like a hand
on my shoulder.

A poem is a needle.

THE GOING

We used to drink
coffee in bed you
and I. Funny it had
never occurred to
me to prop myself
up in the place I
just rose up from.
So many things you
taught me when I
wasn't looking. So
what if we were
lovers and then we
weren't, so what if
I burned for you for
months after. I'll tell
you I never saw it
coming. The going,
that is. Then I rose
up and went to a
different place, not
propped up exactly.
We wore the cost-
umes of trying-to-
be-friends until the
tags came off. Mine
is tucked in behind
old journals, faded
magazines. I wonder
where yours is. I
wonder where you
are now as the sun

just wakes up, no
electric charge in my
chest, just a glance
over my shoulder in
your direction, sitting
with a question.
I learned that from you.
I learned that indirectly
from the leaving.

NOW I'M OLD AND I SEE WHY MY MOM
LOVED CHRISTMAS

What if a gingerbread house
were a metaphor? The hands
that take the time to build
something beautiful are often
the same hands that build
a home. To give time is,
after all, the deepest gift—
not shiny, not tucked neatly
beneath a tree, but instead
nudged in between
its arrow needles in the
strings of light, the popcorn,
the asymmetrical and lumpy
ornaments painted and
shellacked, the toilet paper
roll Santa with cottonball hair.
It's in the plate of
cookies from a recipe in
cursive handed down, in
the songs that become
almost like friends, we can't
remember when we met.
So delicious a door, a window,
entering to feast and to rest,
to take time because it is there,
because we are there, because
we are, for a moment, lit up
by the sweetness of it.
So delicious the comings,
and even the leavings.

In this metaphor you would
eat your life; that sounds
about right to me.

SUGAR BEETS

Sometimes while growing up,
the large people go on and on
and on about cooked roots.
Oh these rutabagas, I CRAVE them!
And beets, oh my! they say as you
turn your head sideways, squinting
like a dog whose food has been moved.
Who are these strange people?
Then later when you are no longer
small you lose things; in the middle
of creating a picture bank of memories,
you build things and watch them
crumble. Sometimes it's the wind
that does it, trickster with a right
hook. In the memory bank here are
those jagged knife Swiss mountains
(you can see Italy from here!),
the dawning notion that borders are
our favorite form of fiction. Here are
the frozen forever fields in Minnesota;
after you make a joke about corn,
your friend says *no, they're sugar beets!*
—Wait, they're made of sugar?—
You build something else, something
with your heartwings, and watch it
dissolve. Oh, this again. Now I see.
This bloodred orb from underground
tastes different now, sudden earth on my
tongue is a revelation. I taste time,
sun, yes, even wind, even pelicans

circling overhead as I realize: this was
inevitable. Roasted with olive oil
and ample salt is what I prefer.

GHOST STORIES

My friend wrote a song
called "Ghosts Are Real"
and I beg him to play it—
the bittersweet rush of regret,
of memory, of nostalgia, his
worn flannel voice like salt
water washing me clean.

He could sing "Sandwiches
Are Real" and both would be
true, but it's not the same.

These days the word ghost
has become a verb, an
extension of itself meant
to describe someone who
doesn't take your call anymore,
who doesn't want to be found.

I've known both kinds, my
grief a seesaw on an empty
playground. Sorrow doesn't
care about parts of speech.

I listen for what moves
in the dark.
I can never get enough.

WITH DOG AS MY WITNESS

Do you accept the Lord Jesus Christ into your heart as your personal savior? asked the father of the merengue bride at the wedding for which I had been hired to sing (by same said father), whose warm breath skirted my neck as he leaned in to whisper and caused my stomach to flip. *I'm all good, thanks* was all I could think to say, which, of course, I wasn't. I had just witnessed a room full of people witnessing a young lamb of a girl promising to obey her husband, also lamb, but slightly meatier and standing on centuries of violence which looked for all the world like a stack of books. Being a poet I'm too busy wanting to know what's in the books. Looking back, I wish I'd reached over him for the salt and poured the whole thing into my mouth. I wish I'd shouldered some space and said *Well sir, thanks for asking, but that's between me and my dog.*

CHEF'S SECRET

You need to be more serious,
said the man who took
himself so seriously his
hair stood up straight to try
and get away from him.
Too many exclamation points,
he said. His words slapped
me in the young face, I took
them back to my cave, chewed
on them, felt the back-of-the-
neck heat of shame over them,
wondered why I can't just be
normal. I even tried amending
my ways but I tripped over a
root and laughed out loud when
I hit the ground; I'm told my
grandmother used to do that
and she was even taller than
I am, she had further to fall.
Only nineteen years later while
mincing onions did I realize
I should have employed a
sharp retort, should have told
him *you need to loosen your grip,*
your trip, ha. Then again if he
were less serious this never
would have happened, never
would have flavored the stew
I am just now making. Now
I feel for that young-faced
old me, knowing I failed her

when I reached out and took
the shame that was not mine.
Can a reflex be forgiven? Time
handed me what was missing.
Turns out she was right to
be delighted by the world;
everything tastes better
that way.

HOW TO FAIL AT CLIMBING

Look down into a turning
abyss that your ears
know but refuse to admit.
Focus on a rabbit down there,
follow a flyover sound,
gawk at clouds that two
seconds ago were not there,
wait a minute, were they?
Remember something someone
important said, place it above
the ringing blue unsaid,
scramble, gasp through
your matchstick teeth, correct.
How to win: start laughing.

LITTLE GENERALS

Funny how things are
rarely as they seem—
the thin, leaky veil slowly
lifted over time, or

suddenly punctured by a
betrayal–the surprise of it
a kind of delicious violence
we learn to wrap around

our shoulders, our stories
to keep us warm by the fire.
Funny how we all have
armies lined up and waiting,

some more well-fed than
others, some bedraggled
and starving, ready to defend
at any moment. The tyranny

of an ill-placed sigh, a slip
in consciousness, a wrong
turn. All of us little generals
shouting from atop our

heaving horses, expecting
absolute victory or if all
else fails, equal surrender.
Anticipating perfect sym-

metry when in fact every last
thing is born of chaos, even
love. You might as well expect
a stone to say your name.

WHEN WOMEN COME TOGETHER

There is the sound of listening.
There is braiding of stories, hair, lives.
There are cups for tea, wine, tears;
there are many dishes piled up.

When women come together
there is feasting, cooking, alchemy,
ancient wisdom meets
what's-on-sale-today.

When women come together
there is work to be done.
We chat, laugh, cry, hold space,
birth something in each moment.

When women come together
we make the world.

POEM AS…

Poem as gate
poem as offering
poem as life raft
poem as rallying cry
poem as surrender
poem as lift
poem as marker
poem as question
poem as change agent
poem as necessary object
poem as whisper
poem as wailing grief
poem as handful of daisies
poem as hope
poem as medicine
poem as song
poem as sanctuary
poem as hammer
poem as soft place to land
poem as deep water
poem as outstretched hand
poem for you.

A CATALOGUE OF TINY MIRACLES

I want to live in a world
where there are high-fives for poetry.
Yesterday's open mic was
a tiny catalogue of miracles:
You say *I'll gather my courage to speak now,*
We say *And I will listen.*
This sacred contract lit up with mercy,
with blunt afternoon sun, the frontrow
teacherpoet slapping the hand of each
brave reader as they floated down
on feathers from the podium.

Our poetry class was
its own catalogue of miracles—
the prompts just on our last day
consisting of:
--Dream Tracing
--5 x 5
--20 Little Poetry Projects
--The 72 Micro-seasons of Japan

You see, now I am collecting things.

And because I cannot stop collecting,
I pause in front of the message board
in the lobby to see what words I find:
--A ride from Boise to Joseph?
--Lost pair of reading glasses, tortoise shell
--Lost small binoculars, no case, unremarkable
--Mini-golf, anyone?

My eyes catch on this one, the record skips:
--Crazy crow lady, please text Mike.

How will I know that I am not
the crazy crow lady?

I jot down his number just in case.

A POET'S HEART

I have a poet's heart
and so I rise early,
my hair a tangled
secret garden
full of birds.
I eat lunch alone
on purpose.
I drive to the park
by the river—
my steps fueled
by grief, hands
outstretched
to singing water.
I never belonged
to the word *wife*;
the word *mother* was
sandpaper, making dust.
I project my longing
six feet ahead like
a shadow, so we dance.
(Or is it six weeks?)
I take everything hard,
sing it like it's easy;
give me a sun-drenched
patch of grass over a
bustling crowd any day—
if I ever grabbed hold
of what I'm reaching for,
I'd give it all away.

HYMN FOR THE NEW YEAR

A year will never
slap you in the face
although it may feel
like it did, your jaw
bruised and aching
like this early winter
afternoon sky.

A year did not ask
to be born,
to be cherished
or disdained,
strung up like party
lights or banished
for good.

A year stands in wide
greenfields mute and
chewing cud, certainly
not judging, studying
patterns and memorizing
its surroundings, slick
yellow coat on a fence
post in the rain.

A year is not yours or mine,
fine or coarse,
deft or clumsy,
does not care where
hair is growing
and where it's not.

Suddenly there is nothing
a year can't do.
I've looked around the
ceiling tiles for the courage
to wait and see.

A year in no hurry clears
its throat, walks into
a room, opens to a page
and starts singing.
I take a deep breath,
pick up my pen,
write the ending.

MEASURING

You could measure a life

by birds or by thumbtacks,

by teaspoons or by river miles.

By children, by memories, by climbing,

by piles and piles of things, shiny or otherwise,

by paintings, houses, ringing church bells,
university degrees,

by words written, words read, words spoken,
whispered or sung.

Isn't it much easier to have something to do with
our hands?

Think of other things you could do with them.

Think of the not-doing you came here with.

Think of the way a body softens with age,

the way tenderness loosens the light.

You could try not measuring at all.

COLOR OF DAWN

If there are still
wild horses when I die,
go to them.
Watch them run.

Then search for the condor:
commodore ever skyward,
fragile, massive and nod
yes, note his feather
on the ground.

Just for kicks watch
an otter turn in green
rippling water, slick
twisting trickster of
bubbling streams.

If it feels like
remembering,
embrace that, listen
if it feels like the color
of dawn.

That is the feeling ever
blooming
when I hear a voice say
goodnight, pumpkin,
and then I sleep.

WAIT RIGHT HERE

A blizzard warning makes
your head a spinning top—
yes, there are eggs, potatoes,
lentils, maybe even kale.
There is coffee, cream, this
checklist dancing around
the upward slope of hours.
One day you will learn
you don't need time, stillness,
even hands to sift through
the glistening sand of your life
for treasures. No howling
winds can touch them, hide
them away. One day, that
golden morning by the river
will save you from sorrow,
will anchor you, will wash
you clean. In darkness,
keep going. Wait right here
for the light.

GRATITUDE

To D, thank you for the verb of our love and for being proud of me.
Thank you, A&B for your encouragement and your belief in me always.
Thank you, fellow poetry lovers and word nerds for sharing my outright giddiness at this form that has nourished my spirit time and again.
Thank you, Clare for the use of your beautiful painting.
Thank you, Sally for making it easy.
Thank you, patrons and friends for your encouragement and support.
Thank you for reading this, for spending a little time here with me.

ALSO BY BETH WOOD

BOOKS:
Believe The Bird
Ladder To The Light
Facepalm: Stories from the Merch Table
Kazoo Symphonies

ALBUMS:
Love Is Onto You
Home By Dark Live with Beth Wood
Deep Blue *(Stand and Sway)*
The Long Road
Spring Tide
Sometimes Love
The Weather Inside
Beachcomber's Daughter
Marigolds
You Take The Wheel
Ghostwriter
Wooden Coyote
Late Night Radio
New Blood
Woodwork

www.bethwoodmusic.com